The author gratefully acknowledges the
support and expertise of Dr. Sheperd Doeleman,
Dr. Peter Kurczynski, and the National Science
Foundation, especially Josh Chamot.

For Sally, Will, Brady, Crowley, and Quinn—
who have the potential to change the world
—A.C.R.

For my dad, who relished
solving the toughest equations
–Y.I.

The Gravity Tree: The True Story of a Tree That Inspired the World
Text copyright © 2021 by Anna Crowley Redding
Illustrations copyright © 2021 by Yas Imamura
All rights reserved. Manufactured in Italy.
No part of this book may be used or reproduced in any manner whatsoever without written permission except
in the case of brief quotations embodied in critical articles and reviews. For information address HarperCollins
Children's Books, a division of HarperCollins Publishers, 195 Broadway, New York, NY 10007.
www.harpercollinschildrens.com

Library of Congress Cataloging-in-Publication Data

Names: Redding, Anna Crowley, author. | Imamura, Yas, illustrator.
Title: The gravity tree : the true story of a tree that inspired the world / by Anna Crowley Redding ; illustrated
    by Yas Imamura.
Description: First edition. | New York, NY : Harper, an imprint of HarperCollins Publishers, [2021] | Audience:
    Ages 4-8 | Audience: Grades K-1 | Summary: "Part scientific explanation, part biography, this nonfiction
    picture book explores the life of the fabled apple tree that inspired Newton's theory of Gravity—from a minor
    seed to a monumental icon that has inspired the world's greatest minds for over three and a half centuries"—
    Provided by publisher.
Identifiers: LCCN 2020011118 | ISBN 9780062967367 (hardcover)
Subjects: LCSH: Newton, Isaac, 1642–1727—Juvenile literature. | Apples—History—Juvenile literature. |
    Human-plant relationships—Juvenile literature. | Gravitation—Juvenile literature.
Classification: LCC SB363 .R38 2021 | DDC 634/.11—dc23
LC record available at https://lccn.loc.gov/2020011118

The artist used Caran d'Ache neocolor ii and Procreate to create the digital illustrations for this book.
Typography by Rachel Zegar
21 22 23 24 25 RTLO 10 9 8 7 6 5 4 3 2 1
❖
First Edition

The GRAVITY TREE

The True Story of a Tree That Inspired the World

WRITTEN BY ANNA CROWLEY REDDING

ILLUSTRATED BY YAS IMAMURA

HARPER

An Imprint of HarperCollinsPublishers

A tree may seem like a rather *ordinary* thing. But hundreds of years ago, a tree was about to embark on an *extraordinary* journey. And it all started with just a speck of a seed. Inside that tiny black shell was enough potential to change the world.

Nestled down in the dirt, the still seed slept—until the warmth of spring saturated the soil. Soaking up water, the apple seed swelled and swelled—until, with a shift and a shake, the seed split its shell.

A wisp of roots webbed down, down, down as a tender shoot tunneled
up, up, up. Then it reached the light. Little leaves fanned out. And they were
full of tiny cells that collected sunshine and transformed those golden rays
into sugary food. It was the perfect fuel for growing bigger and bigger still.

Season after season, the tree
put on a spectacular show.

Golden autumn leaves took to the
wind until bare branches withstood
winter weather.

The tree's tips ballooned with blossoming buds,
swarmed by bees

until petals fell away
to reveal growing apples.

Until bending and bowing, the
tree's branches weighed heavy with
fruit, ripe and ready to fall.

And on one late summer day around 1665, the tree was not alone. Who sat below its canopy? One of the greatest thinkers in history, Isaac Newton. The question-asking, truth-seeking, math-loving Isaac had grown up in the shadow of this tree. And now, the all-grown-up Isaac leaned against the trunk. His mind was full of questions. And the tree was full of apples.

Until—

THWACK!

That **THWACK** sparked an explosion of questions in Isaac's mind!

Why did that apple fall DOWN?

Why not *up* toward the sky?

Why not skitter sideways?

WHY?

Which got him thinking about an even bigger question . . .
Could that falling piece of fruit explain why the moon doesn't
float away from Earth or crash and smash right into it?

Then Isaac came up with the answer: gravity! Universal gravity!
He discovered that the same invisible force that pulled the apple
toward the center of the Earth also kept the moon from drifting
off into space.

This scientific discovery is one of the most important, genius ideas of all time. Isaac's fate was set in motion. And as Isaac became a sensation, so did the tree. It earned a new name: the Gravity Tree.

People wanted to
see the tree, sit under
the tree, taste an apple from
the tree—anything just to be near the tree that
had inspired such greatness!

Even long after Isaac died, his ideas lived on.

And so did the tree.

But one stormy day around 1820, the wind whipped into a ferocious howl. With a

CRACK and a BOOM,

the Gravity Tree crashed to the ground.

Curious crowds carried away wooden shards—small pieces of the tree that had inspired such greatness. An entire branch was even used to make a chair, a perfect perch for pondering.

But as for the Gravity Tree itself? It was a dreadful sight.
A haphazard heap of wood. Alone in the garden. Dead.

But deep inside the fallen trunk . . . part of the tree was still alive!
With water and sunlight and time—new roots formed, drilling deep
down into the dirt. On top of the trunk, a shoot sprouted *up*, thickening
and branching as the tree grew bigger and bigger still.

And once again the Gravity Tree drew crowds.
Then one afternoon in 1930, a strange shadow
appeared under the tree. The shape of a man
with wild and crazy hair poking out from under
his hat.

It was none other than Albert Einstein.
World-famous, Albert was on his way
to give a nearby lecture about his own *big,
huge, important* ideas—that were built on Isaac's
discoveries almost three hundred years earlier.

But first, Albert simply had to see the tree
that inspired his ideas.

And Albert wasn't the
only question-asking
scientist to make
the trip.

Astronauts and astrophysicists and thousands of scientists can trace the beginning of their own scientific journey back to the tree.

On a cold winter day in 1987, the tree once again welcomed another extraordinary thinker. World-famous brilliant physicist Stephen Hawking cast his eyes on the tree that set his own path in motion.

Stephen may have been busy studying black holes, gravity, and the origins of, well . . . everything. But none of his big ideas about the cosmos would have been possible without the tree that dropped the apple that inspired Isaac Newton, which sparked even more discoveries.

Just like that once-tiny speck of an apple seed, Stephen too had the potential to change the world.

The tree's work was not done.

No matter the decade. No matter the century, the tree continued to inspire people all over the world. And beyond . . .

$$\sin x \simeq x - \frac{x^3}{3!}$$

On one spring day in 2010, it wasn't so much *who* was visiting the tree but *where* a piece of the tree was headed!

Three.
Two.
One.
Blast off!

Aboard the International Space Station, an astronaut released a sliver of the Gravity Tree from his grip. The wood did not fall down to Earth; it *floated*. Nearly 350 years later, Isaac was right!

The tree's journey was not over!

A master carriage maker carefully crafted a coach for the queen of England. Sanding and shaping, he used a small piece of the tree to adorn his gilded masterpiece. Now the tree was ready for a royal ride as a crowning jewel!

But for people who could not travel to England to see the living Gravity Tree, how could they be near the tree that inspired such greatness? Expert gardeners had thought of that!

They planted seeds from the Gravity Tree's apples. And they carefully sawed away small branches from Isaac's tree to make *new* Gravity Trees.

After traveling on trains and sailing on ships, the saplings inspired crowds in their new homes around the world.

As for the *original* Gravity Tree, it has grown gnarled and twisted and requires a bit of support, but it's still alive! It still produces apples, just like the one that fell right before Isaac's eyes.

And those expert gardeners take great care of the Gravity Tree and its descendants around the world so that *you* might visit and find inspiration of your own.

A tree may seem like a rather *ordinary* thing. But hundreds of years ago, a tree was about to embark on an *extraordinary* journey. And it all started with just a speck of a seed.

You too may be small. But inside you is enough potential to change the world!

THE GRAVITY TREE

*"If I have seen further it is by standing
upon the shoulders of giants."*

—Isaac Newton, 1675

You can visit the original Gravity Tree outside Isaac Newton's childhood home in England at Woolsthorpe Manor, for it is still standing today. You can also see the room where Isaac worked.

In 2002, Isaac's Gravity Tree was declared a living part of English Heritage along with forty-nine other trees, in honor of the queen's Golden Jubilee. This declaration affords the tree special protection and extra care. Some have wondered if the apple falling from this tree truly inspired Isaac. The story *is* true. Not only did Isaac personally tell people about it, but researchers have used modern technology to date the tree and historic research to identify the tree throughout the centuries. That said, the tale that the falling apple hit Isaac square on the head is not true. He simply saw it fall, no bump on the head necessary!

ISAAC NEWTON

ISAAC NEWTON was born on Christmas Day in 1642, at Woolsthorpe Manor in Lincolnshire, England. Isaac did not have an easy childhood. His father died just before he was born. Then his mother remarried, and Isaac was left to be raised by his grandparents. This made him feel very sad and angry. Even so, Isaac spent his free time building, inventing, and experimenting. Had you stopped by his home, you might have found him telling time with his sundial, making miniature furniture for a friend's dollhouse, or training a mouse to run his miniature flour mill!

Isaac was expected to follow in his father's footsteps and become a farmer. But Isaac didn't care for farming. Eventually his mother gave in and let Isaac go to college at Trinity College at Cambridge University. But she was not interested in paying for his education. So Isaac worked for other students while he kept up with his studies. When the bubonic plague hit London, his university was worried the disease could spread, so the students and staff were sent home. During the next year and a half, Isaac made some of his biggest discoveries. Not only did he figure out why the apple fell from the tree, but he also figured out that white light is made up of many colors, explaining one of the biggest mysteries of his time: rainbows and how they worked. Isaac also developed his famous laws of motion and more.

Eventually he was knighted by the queen of England, becoming Sir Isaac Newton. As for Isaac's discovery about gravity, it became the foundation of physics, and he also developed a type of math called calculus. He died at age eighty-four and was buried next to other famous people in Westminster Abbey, an honor reserved for a very special few.

ALBERT EINSTEIN

ALBERT EINSTEIN came up with the equation $E=mc^2$. It is by far one of the most famous equations in history. It explains the relationship between energy and matter. E stands for energy. M stands for mass, and c stands for the speed of light.

This equation changed everything in the human quest to understand how the universe works. He also determined that the speed of light is constant, and, with his general theory of relativity, Albert explained how time and space are related and that space is moving, not simply a black backdrop for stars and galaxies. This idea came after his careful study of Newton's laws of motion and universal gravity. Indeed, Isaac had established the foundation for modern physics. Albert understood the brilliance of these discoveries and their limitations.

Albert was born on March 14, 1879. Like Isaac, Albert grew up asking questions. He wanted to solve the greatest mysteries of the cosmos. As a child, Albert didn't start talking until much later than other kids. He said that he always thought in pictures first, not words. Albert solved many mysteries and made many discoveries, eventually winning the Nobel Prize. His last name even became another word for "brilliant." Albert died in 1955 in New Jersey.

STEPHEN HAWKING

STEPHEN HAWKING was an important theoretical physicist. His work centered on investigating black holes and the origins of the universe. Not only that, he was a phenomenal science communicator. Sometimes, if you aren't a scientist, the work of astrophysicists is hard to understand. Stephen Hawking changed that by explaining the universe in plain language. His books were wildly popular. One even became an international bestseller.

Born in 1942, Stephen went to the same college Isaac had hundreds of years earlier.

Stephen was diagnosed with the debilitating disease known as ALS when he was just twenty-one years old. Doctors told him he would only live for another two years. But Stephen continued his studies and research, determined to make a meaningful contribution to science for as long as he was alive. Defying all odds, Stephen survived year after year after year. In 1979 he was awarded the very same prestigious job once held by Isaac Newton—Lucasian professor of mathematics at Cambridge. And just outside the building where Stephen worked was a Gravity Tree descendant. Amazingly, Stephen lived to age seventy-six. He died in 2018.

ISAAC NEWTON TIMELINE

1642, Christmas Day—Isaac Newton is born at Woolsthorpe Manor, Lincolnshire, England.

1661—Isaac enrolls at Trinity College at Cambridge.

1665—The plague strikes England. Public spaces and colleges are closed. Isaac is sent home and continues his studies there.

1665–1666—During Isaac's stay at home, he sees the apple fall!

1667—Isaac is back at school.

1669—Not only had Isaac graduated, he continued investigating his big questions. His brilliance did not go unnoticed! He was elected Lucasian professor of mathematics at Cambridge, an honor that will one day be bestowed on Stephen Hawking.

1672—Isaac joined the Royal Society of London, a very prestigious and important scientific society.

1687—Isaac shares his discoveries with the world, including what he learned from the falling apple. It's a theory called universal gravity.

1703—Isaac is elected president of the Royal Society.

1705—Isaac is knighted by Queen Anne. Now you may call him Sir Isaac Newton. Thank you very much!

1727—On March 20, Isaac dies and is buried at Westminster Abbey.

BIBLIOGRAPHY

Anscombe, Charlotte. "Remembering When . . . Albert Einstein Visited the University—and Was Late!" *The News Room* (blog). University of Nottingham, June 5, 2015. http://blogs.nottingham.ac.uk/newsroom/2015/06/05/remembering-whenalbert-einstein-visited-the-university-and-was-late/.

Christianson, Gale E. *Isaac Newton and the Scientific Revolution*. Oxford: Oxford University Press, 1998.

Christofaro, Beatrice. "Stephen Hawking's Daughter Said He Would Have Been 'Blown Away' by the First Image of a Black Hole." *Business Insider*, April 11, 2019. www.businessinsider.com/black-hole-stephen-hawking-blown-away-says-daughter-2019-4.

Ewbank, Anne. "How Isaac Newton's Apple Tree Spread Across the World." Atlas Obscura, June 26, 2018. www.atlasobscura.com/articles/newton-apple-tree.

Keesing, Richard. "A Brief History of Isaac Newton's Apple Tree." University of York, Department of Physics. Accessed March 24, 2020. www.york.ac.uk/physics/about/newtonsappletree/.

Killelea, Amanda. "Queen's New Carriage Made from Isaac Newton's Apple Tree, Nelson's Ship and Dambusters Plane." *Mirror*, June 3, 2014. www.mirror.co.uk/news/uk-news/queens-new-carriage-made-isaac-3641958.

Krull, Kathleen, and Boris Kulikov. *Albert Einstein*. New York: Viking, 2009.

Krull, Kathleen, and Boris Kulikov. *Isaac Newton*. New York: Viking, 2006.

Lasky, Kathryn, and Kevin Hawkes. *Newton's Rainbow: The Revolutionary Discoveries of a Young Scientist*. New York: Farrar, Straus and Giroux, 2017.

Meltzer, Milton. *Albert Einstein: A Biography*. New York: Holiday House, 2008.

Moore, Keith. "Newton's Apple Tree." *The Repository* (blog). The Royal Society, February 22, 2012. https://blogs.royalsociety.org/history-of-science/2012/02/22/newtons-apple-tree/.

National Trust. "Woolsthorpe Manor." Accessed March 24, 2020. www.nationaltrust.org.uk/woolsthorpe-manor.

Redd, Nola Taylor. "Stephen Hawking Biography (1942–2018)." Space.com. March 14, 2018. www.space.com/15923-stephen-hawking.html.